THE PRAIRIE
ROSE
GARDEN

Jan Mather

Red Deer College Press

The Publishers

Red Deer College Press	Red Deer College Press
56 Avenue & 32 Street Box 5005	P.O. Box 468
Red Deer Alberta Canada T4N 5H5	Custer, WA 98240

Acknowledgments

Cover design by Kunz + Associates

Text design by Dennis Johnson

Printed and bound by Everbest Printing Co. Ltd. for Red Deer College Press

Financial support provided by the Alberta Foundation for the Arts, a beneficiary of the Lottery Fund of the Government of Alberta, and by the Canada Council, the Department of Canadian Heritage and Red Deer College.

COMMITTED TO THE DEVELOPMENT OF CULTURE AND THE ARTS

Canadian Cataloguing in Publication Data

Mather, Jan, 1954–

The prairie rose garden

ISBN 0-88995-163-2

1. Rose culture—Prairie Provinces. 2. Rose gardens—Prairie Provinces. 3. Roses—Varieties. I. Title.

SB411.5.C3M37 1997   635.9'33372'09712   C96-910777-3

5 4 3 2 1

*For my mother and sister, with love,
and for all the pioneer prairie gardeners
who dared to dream of taming wild roses*

Acknowledgments

Many talented people assisted in making this gardening book a reality, and I would like to offer my appreciation.

Once again, I wish to extend sincere thanks to Dennis Johnson, publisher extraordinaire of Red Deer College Press, who has been enthusiastic about the idea from the beginning. I would also like to thank Carolyn Dearden of Red Deer College Press who lavished support, encouragement and editorial expertise. Together they have nurtured this book's development. I consider myself fortunate to call them both my friends.

Special thanks are also due James Heeks for capturing the grace and beauty of the rose with his photography; to Allan Sweetser for sharing his ideas and insights, sensitivity to the art and beauty of gardens, and for sharing my obsession with all of it; to Annie Mulligan, Carolyn Rallison, T&T Seeds and Sandy Small for supplying stunning rose photographs; to Ben Kunz and Kendra Jacob Azevedo for providing zone maps and yet another beautiful prairie book cover; to Karyn Wellington for creating wonderful illustrations; to Kathy Hager and Saundra Garden for their continual friendship and sense of humor; to Vicki Mix for her impeccable organization; and to all the prairie gardeners who generously allowed their gardens to be photographed.

Heartfelt appreciation is also extended to my husband for taking over the cooking, cleaning, transporting of children and numerous other domestic chores while this book came to fruition. And to my children, whom I also love and cherish.

—JM

Contents

THE PRAIRIE
ROSE
GARDEN

Hardy Shrub Roses for the Prairies

Roses, with their exquisite satiny petals and compelling perfumes, are unquestionably the most beautiful and coveted flowers in the garden, especially the prairie garden. When you live in a region where harsh, drying winds accompany temperatures of $-40°$, growing tender roses—hybrid teas, grandifloras, floribundas and all their aristocratic cousins—requires more than an aficionado's appreciation of beautiful blooms. If prairie gardeners attempt such roses, they need plenty of rose cones, cumbersome yards of burlap, upside-down cardboard boxes, plastic buckets filled with peat moss and a very optimistic attitude. Without suitable outdoor gear, tender roses do not survive our harsh prairie winters. I know a gardener who once covered her tender roses with all of the above, then added an old ski

The blooms of hardy shrub roses are every bit as sumptuous as tender roses', but they don't require all the fuss and attention.

One of the most versatile of plants, round shrub roses harmonize well in mixed plantings of perennials, shrubs and other roses. If used in a shrub rose bed, they will soften the transition between low- and tall-growing species.

Vase-shaped roses can be planted singly as star performers, as backdrops for shorter-growing perennials and shrubs, or as hedges.

Low-growing roses can be used as borders in flower and shrub beds, planted in rockeries or along pathways, or massed together as colorful ground covers.

Round

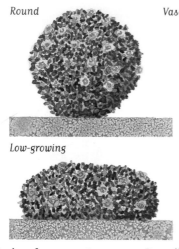

Vase-shaped

Low-growing

jacket for extra insurance. But all her efforts and tender loving care weren't enough; her roses didn't make it through the winter.

The brief growing season of the prairies is challenging enough. Why spend time and energy on ungrateful tender roses? Beautiful roses can be grown on the prairies without paying the price of excessive maintenance if enterprising gardeners choose from the large selection of hardy shrub roses available to them.

Hardy shrub roses are enjoying a renaissance in prairie gardens with good reason. "A rose is a rose is a rose," begins the familiar adage, but not all roses are shrub roses. Shrub roses are deciduous plants with woody upright stems that are sometimes unarmed, but most often prickly. In spring, new growth comes from the roots or lower stems to provide a framework of branches, or canes, defining their individual character. Some shrub

roses develop tall and spindly canes; others stay compact and low-growing. Some develop a full, round appearance, while others develop gracefully arching branches. Regardless of shape, all shrub roses produce lush green compound leaves that decorate their branches all summer and put on a fine autumn display of golden yellow or vibrant russet red.

Shrub rose flowers start the season as slender, sometimes pointed buds in various subtle hues, but soon open to form single, semi-double or double frilly blooms in a variety of sizes. Some shrub roses are delicately perfumed; others are richly pungent. Some flower early in summer; others bloom freely throughout the summer in colors best described as painterly. In the autumn, shrub roses offer an abundance of lingering blooms. To round out the year, unencumbered by a burlap shroud, they decorate the winter garden with colored hips and frost-covered canes.

Rugged shrub roses survive prairie winters with little or no protection because of their breeding. Centuries of hybridizing in Europe have produced an astonishing number of varieties, many of which can be found in the parentage of modern hardy shrub roses. They are derived from species such as *Rosa rugosa*, *Rosa acicularis* and *Rosa arkansana*, which have already mastered overwintering on the prairies. *Rosa rugosa*, for example, is a native of northern China and Japan and has played a vital role in the breeding of hardy roses. *Rosa acicularis* and *Rosa arkansana* are the much-loved prickly wild roses found growing on sunny banks across the prairies. Other species used in the breeding of hardy roses include *Rosa alba*, *Rosa foetida*,

Top: The foliage of prairie hardy shrub roses becomes a colorful pagaent in the autumn landscape.

Left: This cluster of early summer buds will soon burst into an impressive display of seasonal color.

Rosa gallica, Rosa spinosissima and *Rosa kordesii.*

Although its parentage is uncertain, *Rosa alba,* the white rose of York, is reputed to be the first white rose grown by ancient Romans. This famous rose is robust and hardy, pest and disease resistant, and produces an abundance of delicate, semi-double and wonderfully fragrant blooms.

Yellow roses are the hallmark of the species *Rosa foetida.* This native of southwest Asia is commonly called the Austrian Brier rose. Its double form, Persian Yellow, is the parent of nearly all hardy yellow shrub roses.

Garden histories make the claim that the French rose, *Rosa gallica,* has been cultivated since the sixteenth century. This ancient rose boasts a striking combination of flower and foliage. Single, brilliant red flowers contrast their background of deep green leaves. Although its presence in the garden is fleeting, it makes up for this oversight with its lingering perfume.

The species *Rosa spinosissima* was originally found growing in Europe and Asia. Also known as the Scotch rose, this upright-growing shrub produces masses of single white flowers and is one of the earliest to bloom in the garden.

One of the most noteworthy hybridizers from a prairie point of view was Wilhelm Kordes of Germany. *Rosa kordesii,* from rugosa stock, is one of the most important parents of hardy roses. The prolific cultivars Henry Kelsey, John Cabot, John Davis and William Baffin have *Rosa kordesii* in their parentage.

Canadian plant breeders have also contributed significantly to the development of hardy shrub roses. Over fifty years ago, pioneer plant breeders Percy Wright of Saskatchewan, Dr. Frank Skinner of Manitoba, and George Bugnet and Robert Simonet of Alberta began using wild prairie roses in the parentage of new varieties and made available many outstanding roses for prairie gardeners. Their combined successes encouraged the subsequent involvement of Agriculture Canada and the development of a breeding program for winter hardy roses.

Among the cultivated hybrids from Agriculture Canada's research stations in Ottawa, Ontario, and Morden, Manitoba, are the Explorer and Parkland series roses, both excellent choices for their hardiness, recurrent flowering and resistance to disease.

Explorer roses, developed by Dr. Felicitas Svedja, use a selection of species roses, hybrid teas and floribundas. From species roses come improved vigor and winter hardiness, and from modern roses come delicately shaped blossoms and repeat flowering. The first Explorer rose, Martin Frobisher, was introduced to gardeners in 1968. With

fragrant pink flowers on nearly thornless canes and a mature height of about $5 - 6.5'$ ($1.5 - 2$ M), this lovely rose continues to impress gardeners today. In 1974 the cultivar Jens Munk became available. This vigorous rose is one of my favorites, blooming prolifically throughout the summer with ruffly raspberry pink blooms. Two years later the richly fragrant Henry Hudson was introduced. Its pink-tipped buds open to reveal a snow-white display of petals. In 1979 came the David Thompson rose with its abundance of fragrant crimson pink flowers. The list continues with Charles Albanel, John Cabot, William Baffin, Henry Kelsey, John Davis, Captain Samuel Holland, Louis Jolliet, John Franklin, Champlain, Alexander Mackenzie, Frontenac, Simon Fraser and George Vancouver.

Parkland roses are the hallmark of the breeding program at Morden, Manitoba. These roses have also been developed using native prairie roses, such as the Prairie rose (*Rosa arkansana*), and a complex mix of hybrids. In 1962, under the direction

Morden Ruby's ruffled, dark pink blooms represent the finest of the hybridizer's art.

of Dr. Henry Marshall, the first cultivar of the Parkland series was released. With prolific, dark-red satiny petals and its unprecedented vigor, Assiniboine set the standards for hardy shrub roses. The crimson red, semi-double blooms of Cuthbert Grant were introduced in 1967. Adelaide Hoodless, with its rich red flowers, followed in 1975, and the carmine flowers of Morden Amorette followed in 1977. The same year, another red-flowering rose, Morden Ruby, was introduced. Morden Centennial, commemorating the centennial of the Town of Morden, Manitoba, was made available in 1980. Morden Cardinette arrived the same year. In 1988, under the direction of Lynn Collicutt, Morden Blush was released. This unique rose offers gardeners a variety of bloom colors, depending on temperature. In cold temperatures the blooms are soft pink, while in warmer temperatures they range from ivory to white. The following year, Morden Fireglow was introduced. Aptly named, its fiery red flowers bloom abundantly throughout the growing season. The Parkland series also includes Winnipeg Parks, a compact rose that boasts a profusion of blooms with scarlet red petals surrounding bright yellow stamens and dark green foliage.

The Canadian government is no longer as committed to the rose breeding program as it once was. But the pioneering spirit lives on as independent growers and breeders further refine the art of hybridizing roses, ensuring that hardy shrub roses continue to grace the prairie garden.

Aside from their hardiness, another excellent reason for choosing shrub roses over tender roses is their design versatility. Myriad shapes and sizes—ranging from low-growing ground covers to tall, graceful, vase-shaped hedges—make shrub roses amenable to a variety of garden locations. They can be enjoyed bordering a flower bed or rock garden, entwined around decorative arbors, rambling over rustic fences or climbing trellis walls. Shrub roses boast single, semi-double or double blooms in delightful colors from clear white to delicious shades of frothy raspberry and deep magenta. Add lush foliage, winter interest, disease and pest resistance, and design versatility, and you have a hardy shrub rose that deserves a place in every prairie garden.

For prairie gardeners who prefer their shrub roses less cultured and refined, there are several species roses to choose from. Ideal for naturalizing in sunny gardens, these free-spirited roses include the Prairie rose (*Rosa arkansana*), Smooth rose (*Rosa blanda*), Austrian Brier rose (*Rosa foetida*), French rose (*Rosa gallica*), Red-leaf rose (*Rosa rubrifolia*) and the rugosa rose (*Rosa rugosa*). Although they vary in appearance, all are worthy of a second look.

As a garden designer I use shrub roses in virtually all my designs. No other roses combine as much four-season beauty, design versatility and hardiness as these. Although they can be enjoyed in gardens across Canada and the northern United States, I have written specifically with prairie gardeners in mind. This book profiles many hardy shrub roses with in-depth descriptions, design options, planting instructions and maintenance advice that will help make growing roses, the queen of flowers, a rewarding experience.

CHAPTER 1

Designing with Hardy Shrub Roses

GIVEN THEIR LUSH FOLIAGE, sumptuous blooms, fall and winter interest, and many shapes and sizes, it's easy to see why the popularity of shrub roses has increased dramatically over the last few years. Whether planted singly as star performers, massed together in profusion or in a drift weaving summer color throughout a flower bed, shrub roses are one of the most versatile plants available to prairie gardeners. You can incorporate them into existing gardens or design entirely new gardens around them.

But before you begin purchasing roses, it is essential that you develop a plan, and the first order of planning is to assess your garden to determine an appropriate site for your new roses. Ideally, you'll need a location that receives at least six hours of direct sunlight a day and

The versatility of hardy shrub roses makes a designer of every prairie gardener.

🌺 17

Many prairie hardy shrub roses will add color and interest to the fall and winter garden.

by learning a few basic design principles. Whether your taste runs to contemporary or traditional, formal or informal, garden design is the artful arrangement of plants and structures. It is the creative combination of color, texture and form within balanced, rhythmic and proportionate compositions. The process of successful garden design begins with identifying the basic elements used to create beautiful gardens and incorporating them into your rose garden plan.

Though there are no hard and fast rules, garden designers use a variety of lines to achieve specific effects. *Curved lines,* for example, tend to create soft, informal styles, while *straight lines* result in strong, formal designs. *Angles* used in formal or informal designs provide contrast and establish focal points. If you decide to use angles, they should stay within the same angle family: $30 - 60 - 90°$ or $45 - 90 - 180°$.

Once you establish the shapes of borders and beds, you need to consider the balanced distribution of shapes, sizes, textures and colors. *Formal balance* relies on the symmetrical placement of plant material on either side of a central axis and lends itself to traditional designs. Prairie gardeners can emulate these by having parallel beds flank either side of a straight pathway. Placed along the front walkway of a tall two-storey or even a

some protection from the hot afternoon sun to keep the blossom colors from fading. The site will also require well-drained, loamy soil, preferably away from large trees as roses are not good competitors. To reduce fungal diseases caused by overcrowding and poor air circulation, the site must have enough room for the roses to reach their mature size. With these requirements in mind, you can develop a garden design that ensures your new roses will flourish.

Basic Elements of Design

Garden design is not a mysterious art form reserved for experienced gardeners only. You can easily embrace the art of garden making

long, flat bungalow, this symmetrical display will lead the eye directly to the front entrance—the architectural focus of the house. *Informal balance* is asymmetrical and relies on placing unequal amounts of plant material on either side of a central axis while maintaining the overall even distribution of shapes, sizes, textures and colors. Informal rose beds can contain a rich mix of colors and sizes within a variety of curved beds and pathways. Consider, for example, creating an informal look in front of the same two-storey or bungalow. The straight walkway would become curved to produce a meandering effect, and the parallel beds would become more casual, with mixed groups of roses bordering the path.

The best garden designs also take account of the need for **rhythm**, a regularly recurring accent achieved by the repeated use of certain elements, such as color, form and line pattern. Rhythmic accents provide a sense of continuity and structure to the design. Imagine, for example, a large flower bed with one tall, pink shrub rose in the back right-hand corner and one red ground cover rose in the front left-hand corner. These roses are lovely to look at individually, but the design will be strengthened if two more pink roses are added to the back corner, odd-numbered groupings of white roses are added to the middle to soften the transition between heights and colors, and two more red ground covers are added to the front corner. With the dominant lines of the composition going from tall to short, and right to left, a much more emphatic rhythm is created. The odd-numbered groupings of single colors also work in harmony with the design's dominant lines.

Planning your garden also

Planted in an informal bed, shrub roses become ideal companions for a variety of summer-blooming perennials.

Crimson red roses such as these complement a planting of vibrant yellow Asiatic lilies or heliopsis.

requires attention to *proportion*, or the comparative size of plants within the landscape. Plants that aren't in proportion to their surroundings will draw attention to themselves instead of the overall design intention. Although, for example, the ground-hugging Charles Albanel produces lovely satiny red petals, it is not a good choice for hiding the corner of a two-storey house. Taller roses, such as Prairie Dawn or Harison's Yellow, would be better.

Once the basic elements of balance, rhythm and proportion have been developed, you need to consider the effect of texture, form and color within the garden plan. *Texture* refers to the roughness or smoothness, coarseness or fineness

of foliage and flowers. Generally speaking, too many textures in one setting create a chaotic effect, while too few textures create a sense of monotony. Although gardeners usually select shrub roses for their bloom color and form, foliage texture becomes an important consideration when roses are featured as accent plants. Some shrubs, such as rugosa roses (*Rosa rugosa*), have deeply veined and wrinkled foliage, which gives them a rugged appearance. Morden series roses have smoother, glossier foliage. Where to put either one will depend on the effect you want to create. Rugosa roses, for example, blend with plantings of wildflowers and native shrubs and trees but contrast the more refined, dainty blooms and foliage of bellflowers (*Campanula* spp.), lilies (*Lilium* spp.) and peonies (*Paeonia* spp.). Either effect can be desirable; the key is to know why you're choosing one possibility over another.

Form refers to the general shape, or outline, of plants, trees, shrubs and structures. Shrub roses can be tall, round, vase-shaped, pyramidal or oval; they can spread horizontally or vertically. When adding them to an existing plan, keep their mature size and shape in mind. The arching canes of John Cabot, for instance, will reach 6.5' (2 M), but the shrub won't be that tall when you purchase it. To avoid disappointment, ensure you read the label or check the reference chart at the back of this book before planting.

Color can help connect plant material to the structures in your landscape and impart a sense of warmth or coolness to the garden design. Some gardeners prefer a romantic blend of pastel hues, such as the lavender pink of Jens Munk, the delicate pink of Morden Blush and the luminous white of Henry Hudson. Others prefer a bold, riotous blend, such as the fiery yellow of Persian Yellow, the ruby red of Scarlet Pavement and the sizzling orange of Morden Fireglow. With their extensive portfolio of colors, choosing roses for your garden can be daunting. To make effective color choices, use a *color wheel*,

The color wheel helps you visualize color schemes for the garden.

which shows the basic interrelationships of colors. Although the color wheel can inspire or help guide you, your choices should also reflect your personality and creativity.

Any three adjoining colors on the wheel are *analogous* and evoke different emotions and effects. Warm colors—red, red-orange, orange, yellow-orange and yellow—tend to make plants appear closer. Cool colors—green, blue-green, blue, blue-violet and violet—tend to recede or appear farther away. Colors opposite each other on the color wheel—yellow/violet, orange/blue and red/green—are *complementary* and make vibrant, powerful combinations.

To make the most effective use of color in the garden, you need to consider not just flower colors but their bloom times. With careful planning, you can create a succession of colorful blooms throughout the season.

Top Left: Single blooms (up to 12 petals).
Bottom Left: Semi-double blooms (13 to 20 petals).
Top Right: Doubles (more than 20 petals).

Step-by-Step Designing

Beautiful rose gardens don't just happen. They are the result of careful planning.

1. From the list of available roses at the back of this book, create a wish list of shrub roses you'd like to try. To guide your choices, answer the following questions:

❋ What size of shrub roses do you need? Small? Medium? Large?

❋ What color of bloom will best complement your garden?

❋ Do you want a fragrant rose?

❋ What rose shapes will best complement your garden? Low-growing? Round? Vase-shaped? Tall?

❋ Are winter hips and colored bark important to your design?

❋ Do you prefer single blooms, semi-double or double?

❋ Is the rose disease resistant?

❋ Is the rose grown on its own roots or is it grafted?

2. Become familiar with the growing conditions of your site. Survey existing topography, plant material and permanent structures, and record shadows, wind patterns, estimated temperatures and views from various vantages—indoors and out. You may, for example, discover during your site analysis that your backyard is too shady and that your roses should be planted in the front garden. You may also discover that an unsightly section of fence can be hidden behind a row of climbing roses.

3. Create a paper plan to scale. Using graph paper, draw your proposed design and note the exact measurements. If you are creating a new rose garden, keep in mind that it can be any shape, providing that its size is in proportion to its surroundings and in harmony with your overall landscape. Once the size and shape have been determined, draw in any other plant material, such as peonies, lilies, irises, delphiniums, summer shrubbery and annuals. A circle template will help you draw circles to symbolize plant forms.

4. Review your wish list, and select your new roses. Then identify their different colors with colored pencils to help you visualize the distribution of color in your new bed.

5. Review the plan and calculate

how many new plants are required. Simply take the square footage of the area and divide this by the space required by the mature size of each plant. Use this information to create a shopping list to take to the garden center or to place an order with a specialty grower.

Foundation Plantings

An excellent place to assess the potential for prairie shrub roses in your landscape is the front garden. Too often the front yard provides

If you enjoy cutting fragrant blooms for indoor arrangements, position shrub roses near pathways for easy access. Shrub roses with long, arching canes like these offer the refined beauty of tender roses without the fuss.

In the front yard (top left), side-yard (top right) or backyard (bottom), shrub roses can be effectively used in foundation plantings as backdrops, transition plants and borders.

the necessary ho-hum curb appeal with two potentilla, one spirea and a couple of junipers for winter color. Although this planting arrangement may unify the house with its surroundings, it lacks flair and drama.

Today, front gardens have become an integral part of our outdoor living area. Front lawns are being

replaced with interesting garden patios surrounded by wildflowers and herbaceous borders brimming with perennials and a medley of colorful shrub roses. Grouping shrub roses will not only help reduce maintenance, but will provide a wonderful intensity of color and fragrance in the front garden.

When selecting shrub roses to add to your garden's repertoire be sure to consider the rose's mature height and width. As pretty as roses are, they shouldn't hide the peonies or the lilies, or be hidden behind the delphiniums. Small- and medium-sized roses are well suited for enhancing mixed plantings of perennials and shrubs in front gardens. Consider, among others, the white-flowering Henry Hudson. This apple-scented rose will intensify most colors of perennials in the summer garden and provide the requisite form for the winter gar-

den. Pink fanciers will enjoy the raspberry pink blooms of Jens Munk or the soft pink of Morden Blush.

Shrub roses also solve the problem of how to enhance existing foundation plantings. If your junipers, for example, need some summer color, consider a border of low-growing Charles Albanel. Its dark pink roses will be a superb contrast to the evergreen background and will create a striking first impression.

Provided that their height is not restricted and their requirements for sun and good air circulation are met, taller shrub roses are also suitable foundation plants. One of the showiest of these is Thérèse Bugnet, a prairie garden favorite since 1950, with dark pink, fragrant roses and red winter bark. Another pink rose to try is John Davis. Although it needs plenty of space to accommodate its rambling nature, once it

flowers and is covered with ruffled pink blossoms, its free spirit is easily forgiven. This flamboyant Explorer rose will perform as a colorful backdrop for slightly shorter perennials, such as blue and white delphiniums (*Delphinium* spp.), various shades of pink lilies (*Lilium* spp.) and white bee balm (*Monarda didyma*). Or you might try it behind a planting of white potentilla (*Potentilla* spp.) shrubs. With or without colorful companions, John Davis is stunning in the summer garden.

Flower Beds

A second place to consider planting shrub roses is in borders or island beds, where these sociable plants can enjoy the company of other flowers. Consider planting light pink roses near blue irises (*Iris* spp.) or bellflowers (*Campanula* spp.) or among a gathering of dark

Left: The frosted hips of hardy shrub roses add interest and drama to the winter garden.

Right: The graceful cup-shaped buds of this hardy shrub rose will soon adorn the garden with a burst of color and fragrance.

Top Left: For something different in foundation beds, try planting shrub roses instead of junipers and potentillas.

Top Right: Betty Bland is ideal for beds and borders.

Bottom: Plant compact roses in the foreground.

pink Asiatic lilies (*Lilium* spp.). Hardy roses also harmonize well with a rich mix of annuals, such as salvia (*Salvia splendens*), snapdragons (*Antirrhinum majus*) and lavatera (*Lavatera trimestris*).

To maximize the amount of sunlight flowers receive, position the tallest shrub roses in the back of border beds and in the center of island beds. Use midsize varieties of different shapes to soften the transition between heights. Then decrease the height of the plants until the shortest are located in the

foreground. To add interest and drama, choose a variety of heights, forms and colors, and plant odd-numbered groupings to create a balanced, rhythmic and proportionate design. For an informal effect, for example, plant smaller groups of roses in casual drifts, which take the form of curves with exaggerated or pulled ends. Formal designs are also easily achieved by planting small roses in neat, orderly lines. These lines can take the form of straight rows, curves or sharp angles, or you can create a mix of the three to form a popular knot garden. The possibilities are endless.

Low-Maintenance Beds

Shrub roses are well suited for gardeners and commercial property owners looking for seasonal color and interest without a great deal of work and expense. For example, when massed together in a large

bed on a sunny slope, the purple leaf shrub rose (*Rosa rubrifolia*) contrasts well with other plant material, forms an impenetrable barrier, prevents erosion and is surprisingly drought tolerant.

In beds where curb appeal is a primary requirement, groups of low-growing roses fill the bill admirably. When planted *en masse* near people-oriented buildings, for example, their abundant blooms create a remarkable display. Their perfumes are also intensified. Because drama and fragrance are virtues to be savored up close, select a planting site near pathways or benches.

Morden series roses, with their compact growth habit and glorious colors and perfumes, offer some of the best choices for mass plantings. Morden Cardinette puts on a spectacular show of ruby red roses throughout the prairie summer,

Morden Blush shows off pale pink frilly blooms, Morden Centennial produces an abundance of medium-pink blooms and Winnipeg Parks displays medium-red roses that fade to dark pinkish red. All are self-sufficient, and all are prairie hardy.

Although they are a relative newcomer to the prairie garden, the Pavement series roses are also beautiful when mass planted. These rugosa hybrids boast a compact habit of growth, prolific, fragrant blooms in various colors, winter

Top: Round, mid-size roses soften transitions between heights.

Bottom: Free-spirited shrub roses suit informal plantings of mixed perennials, such as Veronica, lilies, bellflower and blanket flower.

and act as beautiful backdrops for other flowers. More importantly for prairie gardeners, few hedges offer the practical and aesthetic benefits of a captivating row of roses.

The Explorer series rose David Thompson makes a stunning hedge with its profusion of large, dark pink to deep crimson double blooms and a mature height of about $3 - 5'$ ($1 - 1.5$ M). If you prefer red flowers, consider a row of John Franklin, which reaches a height of about $4'$ (1.2 M), blooms repeatedly all summer and is breathtaking near dark blue delphiniums (*Delphinium* spp.).

If you don't have the space for a new hedge, consider enhancing the leeward row of shelterbelt shrubs with a row of Thérèse Bugnet roses. Famous for its pink blooms and red winter bark, this rose has become a prairie favorite.

Top: Massed elegantly together, these low-growing Morden roses are ideal for low-maintenance beds.

Bottom: A softly rounded Jens Munk complements the subtle hues of painted daisies, lavender, maiden pinks and cranesbill geraniums.

interest and disease resistance. Chief among their attributes is their tolerance to the salty residue splashed up from winter roads, which makes the Pavement series ideal for roadside beds and borders.

Hedges

A third opportunity for introducing versatile shrub roses into your garden is in hedges. Short or tall, formal or informal, hedges play many roles in the garden. They provide privacy, screen out unsightly views, keep out the neighbor's dog

Arbors, Trellises, Pergolas and Gazebos

Another option for enhancing your prairie landscape is to adorn structures with hardy climbing roses. Few sights are as breathtaking as ruffled roses spilling spicy, fragrant blooms over posts and beams. Although the stems of these so-called climbers lack tendrils or adhesive disks with which to climb, they do develop long, graceful canes that grow upward when supported. Without support, their long canes will droop and fall. With a little help, these tall roses can reach

their potential. Located at the tips of their lanky growth are clusters of perfumed blooms, which, when supported by trelliswork or the columns of arbors, pergolas and gazebos, extend color and fragrance to passersby.

Mixing imagination with practicality, prairie gardeners can use these versatile roses to achieve dramatic effects. When fastened to a support, climbing roses can function architecturally to soften, for example, the hard look of concrete retaining walls. As problem solvers, their luxuriant foliage and clusters of summer blooms can screen off undesirable views and camouflage eyesores. Used as decorations, they can embellish archways and, with a little training, become artful, living fences.

Six hardy shrub roses stand out among the rest as candidates for use as climbers in prairie gardens: Henry Kelsey, John Cabot, John Davis, William Baffin, Captain Samuel Holland and Louis Jolliet. Their long showy canes can be secured against a variety of supports: columns and pillars, wrought iron and trelliswork, fences, retaining walls, chain-link barriers and virtually any other vertical structure.

The Henry Kelsey rose was first introduced to prairie gardens in

These magenta roses sharply contrast the house's white siding, and they create an elegant, perfumed boundary.

When adorned with a graceful mix of long-caned hardy roses and clematis, the arches of a front-yard arbor will shower guests with color and perfume.

1984 by Agriculture Canada. Its vigorous growth, arching branches and vivid red petals contrasting bright yellow stamens, make this rose a summer showstopper. Fasten it against a suitable support near plantings of Croftway Pink bee balm (*Monarda didyma* 'Croftway

Pink'), Purple Haze bearded tongue (*Penstemon fruticosus* 'Purple Haze') and blue Veronica (*Veronica* x 'Sunny Border Blue'). These calypso colors will take your breath away.

Also introduced by Agriculture Canada is John Cabot, one of my favorites. Deep orchid-pink ruffled blooms and bright green foliage grace the arching 6' (1.8 M) branches of this hardy rose all summer long. Besides being fragrant, it is disease resistant, and if you've always coveted a pink climber, John Cabot will not disappoint you. Suitable summer companions for this climber include matching pink lavatera (*Lavatera trimestris*) and snapdragons (*Antirrhinum majus*).

All summer long the John Davis cultivar boasts pastel pink blooms that have a delicate spicy scent. With a mature height of approximately 5' (1.5 M), it is not quite as tall as John Cabot, but can be used effectively as a climbing rose. Try it against wooden pillars and posts, where its dark red canes can provide contrast and winter interest. This rose also puts on a good show behind white nicotiana (*Nicotiana* spp.) or near white-flowering sweet peas (*Lathyrus odoratus*).

Another excellent Explorer rose suitable as a climber is William Baffin, whose mature height reaches 6.5' (2 M). With scrumptious blooms that are best described as frothy, raspberry pink with a vanilla center,

this perfumed rose will change the way gardeners look at shrub roses. Try this hardy variety near a planting of deep purple Jackmann's clematis (*Clematis* x *jackmannii*) or as a backdrop for purplish blue liatris (*Liatris spicata*) and fleabane daisies (*Erigeron speciosus*).

Two newcomers to the list of hardy climbers in the Explorer series are Captain Samuel Holland with medium-red blooms and Louis Jolliet with rosy pink blooms. These rugged roses promise a bounty of colorful fragrant flowers and an impressive resistance to black spot.

Long-caned hardy shrub roses, though not true climbers, can be trained to wrap around vertical supports of arbors and other outdoor structures.

The tall canes of John Cabot are ideal for growing against a rustic arbor or fence.

Ground Covers

A final means of incorporating shrub roses into your garden is as a ground cover. Although it may seem a bit eccentric, there are some wild roses that creep and crawl along sunny slopes while their roots hug tenaciously to rocky soil. Of interest to prairie gardeners are two shrub roses that can be considered admirable ground covers: Charles Albanel and *Rosa Paulii*. When planted in a sunny site in well-drained soil, both are reliably self-sufficient and able to produce a wealth of blooms throughout the gardening season. Besides a splendid show of color, their flowers and foliage add texture, fragrance and visual interest to the garden.

Charles Albanel is a rugosa hybrid that boasts clusters of large, semi-double, medium-red flowers. With a mature height of about 20" (50 cm) and a spread of about 3' (1 M), this hardy shrub rose is easy to incorporate into designs. Its silken petals, for instance, look stunning near a planting of creeping bellflower (*Campanula cochlearifolia*) or Johnson's Blue cranesbill geranium (*Geranium ibericum* 'Johnson's Blue'). The richness of its bold colors are intensified near a planting of white perennials, such as snow-in-summer (*Cerastium tomentosum*), lavender cotton (*Santolina chamaecyparissus*) or Veronica (*Veronica* spp.). For the best effect in a rock garden, plant odd-numbered groups of roses to create a strong sense of rhythm. As summer blossoms fade, the colors of the rockery will be enhanced by a brief show of leaves dressed in autumn hues.

Rosa Paulii is another procumbent rose suitable for use in rock gardens, borders or shrub beds. Clear white flowers make it a suitable candidate for use in a variety of color harmonies. Although its mature height is only about 3' (1 M), it makes up for its diminutive form with a generous spread of about 6.5' (2 M). This delightful shrub rose produces masses of single, fragrant blooms early in the summer, which decrease throughout the remainder of the season. But don't hold this botanic anomaly against it—peonies bloom for only a couple of weeks and we forgive them. Because of its rather large spreading habit, this ground-hugging rose needs to be carefully situated. If space allows, plant it to create a meandering ribbon of textural interest between dark pink maiden pinks (*Dianthus deltoides*) and blue bellflowers (*Campanula* spp.). In the flower bed, plant this rose near blue bearded irises (*Iris* spp.) such as Honky Tonk Blues and Sapphire Hills, my two favorites. The effect is dazzling.

CHAPTER 2

Choosing and Buying Hardy Shrub Roses

ARDEN CENTERS AND NURSERIES across North America sell an extensive selection of hardy shrub roses suitable for prairie gardens. Catalogues begin arriving in early January filled with pictures of inspiring blooms and enchanting colors. But how do you choose from among all those lovely roses? Keep in mind that not all roses are hardy. Most reputable companies suggest hardiness zones for their plants to guide your choices.

The prairie climate offers unique challenges, so it is important to be aware of the climatic conditions in your area. Climatic zones are based on the length of the frost-free period, the average minimum temperatures of the coldest months, the average amount of snow cover and the effect of the wind. Though climatic zones are guidelines only and vary from province to province and

Shrub roses can be purchased at your favorite garden center or nursery in pots or as bare-root bushes.

Roses grown on their own roots produce multiple buds and blooms against a backdrop of lush green foliage.

state to state, generally the prairies have a short growing season with moderate to low rainfall and severe winter temperatures. The prairie climate represents six of ten possible growing zones. Variations within a zone are identified with the letters a, b and c. The list of prairie hardy

shrub roses at the back of this book will also help you select an appropriate rose for most Canadian and American prairie gardens. To avoid disappointment, take a few minutes to locate your growing zone on the following zone maps before you place your order.

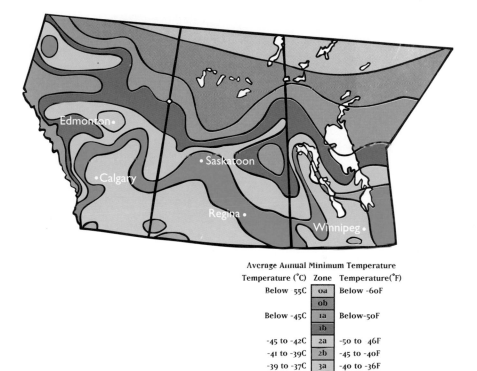

Average Annual Minimum Temperature

Temperature (°C)	Zone	Temperature(°F)
Below 55C	0a	Below -60F
	0b	
Below -45C	1a	Below-50F
	1b	
-45 to -42C	2a	-50 to 46F
-41 to -39C	2b	-45 to -40F
-39 to -37C	3a	-40 to -36F
-36.9 to -35C	3b	-35 to -30F

Average Annual Minimum Temperature

Temperature(°C)	Zone	Temperature(°F)
-42.8 to -45.5	2a	-45 to -50
-40.0 to -42.7	2b	-40 to -45
-37.3 to -40	3a	-35 to -40
-34.5 to -37.2	3b	-30 to -35
-31.7 to -34.4	4a	-25 to -30
-28.9 to -31.6	4b	-20 to -25
-26.2 to -28.8	5a	-15 to -20
-23.4 to -26.1	5b	-10 to -15

The amended soil around this rose provides nutrients for producing full blooms and rich green foliage.

Own-Root versus Grafted Roses

When shopping for shrub roses, you will notice that they are sold as own-root or grafted roses. An own-root rose has been propagated by rooting a cutting from a parent plant and as such does not have a bud union, or graft. On the other hand, grafted shrub roses are grown on rootstock.

Own-root roses are the best choice for prairie gardens for several reasons. First, they are truer to form and color than grafted roses. The process of grafting roses to rootstock sometimes changes the size and color of the blossom and the number of petals. Second, roses grown on their own roots are hardier and live longer than grafted roses. After many years of growth, the bud union of a grafted rose becomes large and swollen, and the general health of the plant declines. Third, own-root roses are less prone to viral invasions because they have no rootstock from which to acquire viruses. Lastly, there are no suckers to contend with when you grow own-root roses.

Selecting Healthy Roses

Shrub roses can be purchased at nurseries or garden centers in pots or as bare-root bushes. Potted roses are usually more expensive than bare-root, but they do provide instant color. Select a specimen for its sturdiness and robust green leaves. If it has plenty of buds and blooms, inspect them closely for signs of insect damage. Check the bottom of the pot for roots growing through the drainage holes. This could be a sign that the rose has been growing too long in the container.

If you select your roses from a specialty mail-order grower, they will arrive in spring as bare-root specimens wrapped in shredded paper or packaged in a waxed cardboard container. Remove the rose from the packaging material and check the roots for damage. The rose

should have plenty of long fibrous roots. Healthy bare-root roses have at least three strong, thick, unblemished canes about $15 - 18"$ $(38 - 45$ cm) long. If pith is visible, it should be white or green, not beige or brown. Buds should be dormant, but if they have started growing shoots, they should be small. Bare-root roses are only planted in spring. If the weather does not permit planting, packaged bare-root roses can be safely stored a few degrees above freezing for about two weeks. Water if necessary.

CHAPTER 3

Planting and Caring for Hardy Shrub Roses

Growing healthy roses on the prairies requires more than simply digging a planting hole and covering the roots with soil. Like other landscaping plants, roses must be thoughtfully positioned if they are to perform successfully.

Your garden's unique microclimate will determine the most suitable location for your shrub roses. The amount of available sun, shade cast by existing trees and structures, prevailing winds and resulting tunnels, and soil types and conditions are all factors to consider. If you study your garden's microclimate carefully and make decisions appropriately, you will be rewarded with enchanting summer blooms. Although shrub roses are tough and forgiving, a little extra effort at planting time will help them reach their full potential.

Blooming effortlessly, the flowers of hardy shrub roses are easy-care sensations in any prairie garden.

With at least six hours of sunlight, this delightful, compact shrub rose will produce an abundance of flowers throughout the season.

Selecting a Site

Whether you are planning an extensive rose garden or adding roses to an existing flower bed, choose a site that receives adequate sunlight, drainage and air circulation. All roses require a minimum of six hours of direct sunlight a day to thrive. Sunlight is the essential ingredient for the production of flowers. Roses grown in partial shade will be spindly and less generous with their blooms. If you are growing roses for floral arrangements, plan to provide for some afternoon shade to help keep the blossom colors from fading. A site that receives morning sunshine will ensure that your roses dry off quickly, reducing the risk of moisture-loving fungal infections.

Roses enjoy an open but partially sheltered location. When selecting your site, keep in mind that roses are not good competitors and should not be planted too close to large trees. Also, avoid planting roses in low spots, where water pools after a rain. Although hardy shrub roses are impervious to cold and neglect, they don't care for wet feet.

Soil Preparation

Like all other plants, roses require balanced nutrition for growth and development. The easiest way to provide these necessary nutrients is with healthy soil. Well-drained, fertile, loamy soil is ideal. But soil zones across the prairies vary dramatically, as do soil conditions from garden to garden. It is essential that you examine your garden's soil.

Soil has two properties that prairie gardeners should be aware of: texture and structure. Soil texture refers to the relative percent-

ages of sand, silt and clay present. The higher the clay content, the heavier the soil. Avoid planting roses in heavy clay soils because their roots will become water-logged. Conversely, sandy soils are so light that they fail to retain water and nutrients.

Soil structure refers to the arrangement of the various soil particles. In ideal topsoil, they are arranged in groups of various sizes and shapes. This mixed bag of soil particles allows for improved water drainage.

Wise gardeners examine their soil closely before making the necessary amendments. If water pools around the base of existing plants, you may need to move them to a temporary location until you can fix the problem of poor soil texture and structure.

Thankfully, soil is the one ele-

ment most amenable to change. Both sandy and clay soils can be made more workable and productive with the addition of valuable soil conditioners, such as well-aged manure, compost and damp peat moss. Combining good drainage with the nutrient and water-holding capacity of these organic substances creates healthy soil for your roses.

If you are planning a new bed for your shrub roses, prepare it early so the soil has time to settle. If possible, prepare the bed in the fall for spring planting. Be sure to incorporate plenty of organic material into the bed so that accompanying perennials and shrubs can benefit too. Add enough growing medium to raise the soil level several inches higher than the surrounding elevation to ensure better viewing as well as improved drainage.

Left: Select locations away from the root systems of large trees; roses are not able to compete for nutrients.

Right: Well-drained soil and a sunny site produce healthy blooms and foliage.

Left: The planting hole for potted roses should be as deep as the height of the pot. Remember to remove the container or wrapping once you've tested the hole's depth.

Right: When planting bare-root roses in the garden, ensure that the graft union is 4 – 6" (10 – 15 cm) below the soil surface and the roots are spread evenly over the center mound.

Planting Bare-Root and Potted Roses

The best time to plant bare-root roses on the prairies is between late April and mid-May.

1. Dig a hole that allows at least 4 – 6" (10 – 15 cm) of space around the root ball. The graft union on grafted roses should be at least 4" (10 cm) below the soil line. Own-root roses should be approximately 2" (5 cm) below the soil line. Long-caned roses planted against vertical supports should be placed in a hole that slopes away from the support foundation.

2. Fill the hole one-third full with amended soil: equal parts of peat moss, perlite or vermiculite, and garden loam.

3. Shape this soil into a cone in the bottom of the hole. To encourage strong root development, mix a generous handful of bone meal or superphosphate into the cone.

4. Place the roots over the mound so they fan out with no restriction.

5. Fill the hole three-quarters full, gently tamping with each addition.

6. Water thoroughly to remove air pockets.

7. Once all the water has been absorbed, completely fill the hole with soil.

8. Create a saucerlike depression around the plant for efficient water absorption.

9. Label a wooden, plastic or metal stake with the cultivar name, and record planting date and cultivar name in your favorite prairie journal.

Left: Decorative containers allow even the smallest of prairie gardens to flourish on balconies, decks, patios and steps.

Right: When planting hardy roses against a wall be sure to dig the hole far enough away from the wall's base to allow for unrestricted root growth.

Potted shrub roses can be planted throughout the growing season as long as the danger of spring frost has passed. Choose a cool, cloudy day to reduce transplant shock.

1. Water the rose thoroughly before you dig the planting hole.
2. Dig a hole as you would for bare-root roses. To ensure the hole is deep enough, place the still-wrapped plant in the hole to check that the top of the container is level with the top of the soil.
3. Remove the rose from the container and break up the root ball a little with your hands to ensure that the roots will grow into the surrounding soil. This is especially important if the rose has become root bound in the pot.
4. Place the rose in the hole, fill the hole with soil and tamp carefully.

5. Create a saucerlike depression around the plant for efficient water absorption and water thoroughly.
6. Label with the cultivar name, and record the cultivar name and planting date in your favorite prairie garden journal.

Planting Roses in Decorative Containers

Growing shrub roses in containers allows you to arrange and rearrange the smallest of outdoor garden rooms at whim. Whether tucked beside your favorite chair on a patio or elegantly framing an entryway, these movable displays are versatile design components.

A variety of containers can be used, from wooden tubs to plastic or clay pots, provided that they

correct growing height. If the rose was purchased in a nursery peat pot, plant it at the same height that it was previously growing. If the rose is bare-root be sure the graft union is at least 2" (5 cm) below the soil surface.

3. Continue adding soil, leaving a bit of watering space at the top of the pot.

4. Plant a few cascading annuals such as lobelia *(Lobelia erinus)* or alyssum *(Lobularia maritima)* with your rose for additional summer color.

5. Tamp the soil firmly and water thoroughly to eliminate air pockets.

6. Place the containerized rose in a sunny, sheltered location that receives at least six hours of daily sunlight.

7. Keep evenly moist during the growing season.

8. The easiest way to overwinter roses in containers is to remove the rose from the container in early autumn and plant it in the garden, where it will receive some snow coverage. When the soil warms up in spring, uncover the rose, replant it in a container and return it to a sunny site.

Feeding

Unlike hybrid teas, floribundas and other tender roses, hardy shrub roses do not depend on chemical rose fertilizers. If you ask prairie gardeners for the secret to success-

When planting bare-root roses in containers, be sure that the roots are spread over the center mound and the graft union is below the soil surface.

have plenty of drainage holes in the bottom. Clay pots should be soaked for about thirty minutes before receiving plants.

Some small preparation is necessary before planting. Use a ready-made soil-less mix or a growing medium consisting of about three parts sandy loam to one part organic matter. Avoid using soil straight from the garden because it may contain unwanted parasites. Excessively long roots may be trimmed to fit the containers, if necessary.

1. Depending on the size of the container, add a couple of inches of coarse drainage material, such as pea gravel, to the bottom.

2. Add a few scoops of soil to the container and set the rose at the

ful rose gardening, virtually all will have the same response: compost. Compost amends the drainage of clay soil, improves moisture retention in sandy soil, provides necessary nutrients to enrich soil, helps sustain healthy plant life and has become one of the best natural alternatives to chemicals.

Each spring, once the temperature has warmed up, apply a spadeful of compost around the base of your roses. A compost topdressing continues to break down, slowly releasing nitrogen and other life-sustaining elements into the soil. A mulch of compost also retains moisture, reduces weeds and reduces soil temperature on hot summer days.

Making Compost

Compost is easily started in homemade or commercially available containers.

1. If you have a container, begin with your stockpile of healthy prunings saved in early spring or with any uninfested branches or twigs lying around.

2. Add a layer of good garden soil or well-rotted manure.

3. Add a layer of organic kitchen garbage, such as vegetable cuttings, leftovers, coffee grounds, egg shells and discarded fruit parts.

4. Alternate layers of garden soil with kitchen refuse, lawn cuttings, leaves and other organic debris. Poke the pile occasionally

Besides providing nutrients for the production of healthy blooms, compost helps keep soil moist and weeds at bay.

Regular shallow weeding keeps weeds from establishing a foothold in the garden.

to aerate it, but don't turn the layers unless the weather is warm.

5. Keep adding material throughout the season. The compost pile will warm while the components decompose. Offensive odors indicate that the compost is too wet, so turn the layers to dry them a bit.

6. Once the compost cools, in about eight weeks, it is ready for use. If quantities of compost are limited, add spadefuls of it around your roses and favorite perennials, where it will do your plants the most good.

If you don't have the space for a composter, you can improve your soil quality with packaged, easy-to-

use sheep, cow and poultry manure, or with bonemeal, fish emulsion and seaweed. Although they can be costly, they are readily available from you local garden center.

Weeding

"A weed is a plant whose virtues have not yet been discovered," noted a wise gardener a century ago. With or without virtues, weeds are tough survivors. They compete for nutrients, water and light, and if you turn your back on them for too long, they will overwhelm your roses and turn the garden into a tangle of rank prickly growth.

A well-tended rose garden, one that offers optimum conditions for growth, will have fewer pests and diseases than a garden filled with weeds. A relaxed attitude toward the diverse flower shapes of unwanted plants is fine, but if you think of weeds as places for annoying insects to overwinter, the motivation to weed regularly will improve. Think of weeding as an opportunity to appreciate the finer qualities of your roses close at hand. Silken petals, compelling perfumes and delightful color are meant to be enjoyed. You may enjoy your roses so much that you start weeding a small portion each day, though a thorough weeding once a week is usually sufficient for most gardens. The key is to remove weeds when they are young, before they go to seed.

Regular shallow hoeing will disturb fewer weed seeds resting below the soil surface. Hoeing too deeply will bring them above ground, where they will germinate.

Watering

Although many hardy shrub roses are drought tolerant, providing a constant moisture supply is important when you establish new roses. Give them the equivalent of at least $1-1.5"$ $(2.5-4$ cm) of water a week. Using a soaker hose, apply the water directly to the soil as wet foliage is susceptible to such diseases as black spot, rust and powdery mildew.

A large watering can also works well. Fill the saucerlike depression around the base of each rose several times. With this method, you will be directing plenty of water to each rose's root system, where it is needed most.

Deadheading

Some shrub roses bloom early in the season in company with bearded irises and peonies. Others prefer to usher in midsummer perennials, such as Asiatic lilies and bellflowers. And then there are recurrent roses, such as Morden Centennial, which bloom effortlessly all summer. Regardless of bloom time, some shrub roses turn into unsightly brown clumps when they have finished flowering. Removing these dead or spent flowers through

To obtain spectacular blooms such as these, ensure newly planted roses receive approximately 1" (2.5 cm) of water a week. Once established, shrub roses are not as thirsty and will tolerate periods of benign neglect.

Regular deadheading keeps a shrub's appearance neat and redirects energy into the production of new blooms.

capable of producing an abundance of flowers without the spent flowers being removed. Keep in mind, though, that when you remove all the spent flowers, you could be removing future rose hips, which add considerable interest to the prairie winter garden.

If you are trying both to increase the number of blooms and tidy up your rose, a compromise is in order. Deadhead some of the spent flowers by cutting the stem just above the second or third set of leaves below the cluster of roses. Using clean sharp pruning tools, cut at a 45° angle just above an outward-facing bud.

Cutting and Drying Blooms for Indoor Use

The charm and fragrance of roses isn't limited to the outdoor garden. Roses enhance any decor, whether simply arranged as single blooms floating in glass bowls or as more elaborately designed summer bouquets. The flowers and hips can also be dried to provide decorations and gifts. An abundant supply of single, semi-double and double flowers can be obtained throughout the growing season from even the smallest of prairie gardens. But a few guidelines are in order.

deadheading improves your garden's aesthetic appeal and channels energy from unwanted seed production to the development of new growth and more blooms.

Not all shrub roses need to be regularly deadheaded. Occasionally, a branch or two becomes unruly and a little tidying is in order. Recurrent roses, for example, are

Some shrub roses, such as Thérèse Bugnet, make it easy to cut blooms. Its ruffled flowers are located at the tips of thornless stems. Not all roses are as considerate.

The best time to cut roses depends on your hectic schedule. Roses cut from your garden in the early morning, before the dew evaporates, are well supplied with water. Roses cut in the early evening take advantage of high sugar reserves produced throughout the day, which go a long way toward maintaining freshness in your arrangement.

For longer-lasting flowers, select blooms that are barely opening. To avoid weakening the plant, do not cut more than one-third of the flowering branch. Use clean, sharp pruners to cut a $45°$ angle just above an outward-facing bud. Cut the stem just above the second or third set of leaves below the cluster of roses.

Flower arrangements will look fresher and last longer if they have been conditioned, which involves filling flower and leaf tissues to capacity with water. Shrub roses require special treatment before they are conditioned or they will not absorb water effectively. With a sharp short-bladed knife, make a 1 – 3" (2.5 – 7.5 cm) split up from the base of the stem. Then split it crosswise to expose even more water-absorbing surface. Some gardeners advocate pulverizing the stem ends with a hammer to achieve the same effect. This may increase absorption at first, but the crushed tissues quickly become susceptible to bacterial decay.

Once you have slit the stem ends, the conditioning process can begin.

Immerse the cut stems loosely in a clean container of tepid water. Leave the flowers in a cool dark place for several hours or overnight. Darkness causes the tiny pores in the leaves and stems to close, reducing moisture loss. The next morning cut the stems under water and remove foliage below the water line. Now arrange your cuttings in your favorite vase or container.

If your roses are newly planted, give them a chance to get established before you remove more than one or two flowers. Be sparing in the amount of foliage you cut with your blooms too. Keep in mind that it takes about seven leaves to manufacture enough energy to produce a single flower.

When cutting blooms for indoor use, snip the stem just above the second or third set of leaves below a cluster of roses.

Top Left: Floating in a glass bowl, these perfumed blooms would make a stunning display.

Top Right: For long-lasting blooms, place roses in a bucket of tepid water immediately after cutting.

Bottom: The perfect blooms of Morden Cardinette will make even the plainest of vases part of a luxurious arrangement. To enjoy these stunning flowers year round, try air drying them for everlasting bouquets.

Because shrub roses have thick, woody stems and present a different look than traditional long-stemmed tender roses, you might want to explore other floral design possibilities, such as decorating indoor wreaths or swags. Flower buds and blooms of shrub roses can also be preserved for dried arrangements, potpourris and stringing on the Christmas tree.

Air drying is the easiest method for preserving your shrub rose blooms. To air dry them, simply tie the short woody stems in small bunches and hang them upside down in a dark dry place with good air circulation. If you are collecting rose petals for creating potpourri, dry them for about a week on a paper towel.

Pruning

The purpose of pruning roses is to moderate nature's course by removing the old shoots to encourage the production of new growth and prolific blooms. Weather permitting, the best time to prune hardy shrub roses is after they start to leaf out in spring, about late April to mid-May.

If you are unsure of how to prune your shrub rose, begin by stepping back from your subject. Bear in mind the natural form of the species. Is your rose a tall wiry climber, such as the pink cultivars John Cabot and William Baffin? Or is it a rounded shrub, such as the

Pink roses and baby's breath are delicate eye-catching companions in the summer garden and the vase.

delightful lavender pink Jens Munk? Work with the natural growth pattern to achieve a harmonious effect. Overzealous pruning, without consideration to the rose's natural shape, will lead to disappointing results.

Although most prairie shrub roses bloom on new wood, there are some that bloom on old wood—Persian Yellow, Harison's Yellow and Austrian Copper, for example. Take care not to remove more than one-third of their old wood or you will have a disappointing show of blooms.

To prune roses you will need proper tools. Use good quality, sharp, scissor- or anvil-style pruners to remove rose canes. Do not use jagged saws or chain saws. If you are trying to tame an overgrown rose that has very thick branches, use long-handled lopping shears and amortize the pruning over three years. Removing more than one-third of the overall size puts a great deal of stress on the rose. Thick gloves and a long-sleeved jacket will protect you from prickly thorns.

Prune to create an open center, which provides good air circulation and reduces the possibility of fungal diseases.

To improve air circulation, create an open center by pruning out discolored dead wood.

Step-by-Step Pruning

1. Begin pruning by removing any damaged, diseased or dead wood. Cut back to wood that shows white or greenish pith.
2. Remove crossed, twiggy or weak side growth. If any canes originate from below the bud union,

When pruning shrub roses, use sharp pruning tools to cut on a 45° angle slightly above an outward-facing bud.

Too Long Too Ragged Correct

which is the swollen graft section below the soil surface, these should also be removed. Using thick gloves, pull the suckers as they appear. If pulling is not successful, dig a small hole at the base of the plant and cut the sucker off flush with the root. If you bought own-root roses, you won't have to worry about removing suckers.

3. Roses enjoy good air circulation. To encourage an open-center habit, cut .25" (8 mm) above an outward-facing bud on a 45° angle. This reduces the likelihood of diseases such as black spot and powdery mildew, which thrive under stagnant air conditions. An open center also allows light to reach all the leaves.
4. When you have finished pruning, remove the cut canes from the garden to reduce the possibility of spreading diseases.

Propagating

Propagating with stem cuttings is a relatively easy and economical way of increasing your collection of roses. Better still, roses propagated in this manner will be identical to the plant from which the cutting is taken, ensuring that its special qualities are uniform in your garden.

There are two types of stem cuttings: hardwood and softwood. Hardwood cuttings are taken when the wood is dormant; softwood cuttings are taken when the wood is actively growing, in spring and summer. Softwood cuttings are best for propagating roses on the prairies.

1. In late spring or early summer, when roses are actively growing, select the rose you wish to propagate. Choose healthy roses that are free of insects and diseases.

2. Using a clean sharp pruning tool, cut $4 - 8"$ ($10 - 20$ cm) from the growing tip of a stem. Remove any flowers or flower buds and put the stems in a small bucket of tepid water.

3. When you are finished cutting the rose stems, remove the cuttings from the bucket of water, dip their base in rooting hormone powder, readily available at gardening centers, and shake off any excess.

4. Insert about one-half the length of softwood cuttings into a pot or container of damp growing medium composed of four parts perlite to one part peat moss.

5. Insert two 12" (30-cm) stakes into the soil to support a clear plastic bag. Place the container in the bag and seal it with an elastic band to create a greenhouselike climate. Place the stem cutting in a bright place but away from direct sunlight.

6. If possible, place your cuttings where they will receive heat from below the pot, such as heat from hot-water pipes.

7. Keep adequately moist, but do not saturate the cuttings.

8. Remove the plastic bag and stakes after new growth begins, usually after five to eight weeks.

9. Transplant cuttings to larger pots and place them outdoors, where they will receive partial shade and protection from the wind until they have had a chance to acclimatize, in about two weeks.

10. Plant your new roses in their permanent location in the garden. Create a saucerlike basin around the base of the roses. Water thoroughly to eliminate air pockets. Label and record in your journal.

CHAPTER 4

Identifying and Controlling Common Rose Pests and Diseases

ROSES DIFFER IN THEIR RESIS-
tance to pests and diseases.
Even the hardiest occasionally
falls victim to unwanted predators.
The best defense against such invasions is to provide optimum growing
conditions—strong healthy plants
are much better equipped to with-
stand certain pests and diseases
than neglected specimens. First and
foremost, buy healthy plants. After
this, select planting sites that receive
plenty of sunlight and air circulation.
Keep your garden clean. Rake up and
destroy fallen, diseased leaves and
prunings to reduce infestations.

Careful siting, quality soil and good air circulation will go a long way in helping to prevent invasions from pests and diseases.

Inspect roses regularly for early
signs of problems, and learn to
identify the guilty culprit. Common
pest symptoms included swollen
stems (called galls), discolored or
spotty leaves, buds with holes, buds
that fail to open and fine webs on
the undersides of foliage. Common

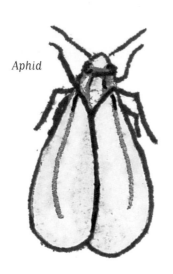

Aphid

disease symptoms include round black spots on leaves, powder or mold, tumorlike growth on the canes, sunken areas on branches or pale yellow spots on leaves.

Although the insects responsible for pest symptoms look menacing, especially when they are drawn many times their actual size, they are usually easily controlled by simply removing them with a gloved hand. Others can be dislodged from their hideouts with a forceful spray of water from the garden hose. Before you arm yourself with chemicals, think about the results of your actions. Chemical warfare indiscriminately destroys good and bad bugs. Why use toxic chemicals when safer choices exist? The first step in adopting an environmentally safe approach to gardening begins with accepting insects as part of the gardening experience. We need insects to pollinate our roses and aerate the soil in which they grow. The second step is accepting slightly less than perfect blooms.

If the idea of removing bugs with a gloved hand makes you squeamish, consider enlisting the help of one of nature's best predators: birds. In return for a nest or perching site, birds will eat their own weight in insects every day.

Not all insects wreak havoc on roses. Some, such as ladybugs, prey on aphids and are beneficial to the garden. A better understanding of pests and diseases is your best weapon for controlling them.

COMMON PESTS
Aphids

DESCRIPTION: Aphids are small, $1/10"$ (2 mm), pear-shaped, soft-bodied insects usually found on the undersides of leaves. They are generally pale green, but some are yellow, brown, pink or black. Aphids cluster in colonies on petals, new shoots and leaves. Adult aphids may be winged or wingless.

DAMAGE: Nymphs and adult aphids damage roses by puncturing the leaves with their mouths and sucking the plant fluids. This causes yellowing, curling and swelling of leaves, flower loss, stunted growth and gall formations on foliage and stems. As aphids feed they excrete a sticky residue called honeydew. Several species of aphids are also capable of spreading fungal and viral diseases.

LIFE HISTORY: Aphids overwinter on the prairies as hard-shelled eggs on the stems of roses. In spring these eggs produce small female nymphs called stem mothers. Within days, the stem mothers give birth to live female nymphs, which in turn give birth to live female nymphs. Twenty to thirty generations are produced in this manner during the summer months. In the fall a generation of winged male aphids is produced. They mate with females, which lay the overwintering eggs.

ECO-FRIENDLY CONTROL: Regularly hose down plants with a forceful spray of water from the garden hose to reduce infestations. Another easy method of controlling aphids is to introduce lady bird beetles, which enjoy feeding on aphids. Lady birds can be purchased from companies that specialize in biological controls.

Rose Curculios

DESCRIPTION: Rose curculios, or snout weevils, are about .25" (8 mm) long, and have hard bodies and a bright red back and black underside. They also have a black head and long black snout with a pair of elbowed antennae.

DAMAGE: Adult weevils pierce sepals and petals with their snouts. Petals and buds become covered with tiny holes, turn brown and fail to open. Damage is also caused by the larvae, which feed on rose hips.

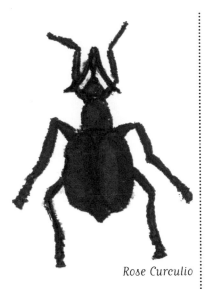

Rose Curculio

LIFE HISTORY: Rose curculios produce one generation each year. Larvae overwinter in earthen cells in the soil around the base of roses. In spring the larvae pupate. Adult weevils emerge in June, about the time when roses are in bud. The adults then begin a feeding frenzy on the buds in an attempt to get at the pollen. After mating in July, the adult female chews holes in the hips of the rose flowers and lays a single egg. Small, white, legless grubs hatch and feed inside the hip on the developing seed. In the fall mature larvae leave the hips and drop to the ground in preparation for overwintering.

ECO-FRIENDLY CONTROL: Adult rose curculios can be removed from infected roses with a gloved hand and destroyed. Removing infested rose hips will also prevent the injurious larvae from hatching and thus reduce the problem in subsequent years.

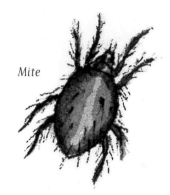

Mite

Mites

DESCRIPTION: The two-spotted spider mite is the most commonly encountered mite causing damage to prairie roses. Mites are very difficult to see without the help of a magnifying glass. They are closely related to insects, but have only two body parts. Their body is oval-shaped and yellowish or greenish with two dark spots on the back. They do not have wings and must walk or be carried by the wind to a new host.

DAMAGE: Mites pierce the epidermis of the leaf and remove the plant fluids. As a result, rose leaves become speckled or spotted, and as damage worsens, they eventually turn pale yellow or bronze. Leaves may dry up and drop from the plant. Leaves closest to the ground are usually the first to be victimized. A close inspection of these leaves and stems will reveal the fine webbing indicative of an infestation.

LIFE HISTORY: Generally, mites overwinter under bark or leaf litter near roses in all stages of development. In spring, when foliage appears on the plants, mites become active. After mating, female mites lay eggs on the lower leaf surface. Summer generations of nymphs may complete development in about a week. Hot, dry conditions are conducive to rapid reproduction. In the fall, overwintering females develop and search for shelter for the winter.

ECO-FRIENDLY CONTROL: During the growing season, control two-spotted spider mite infestations by frequently hosing down roses with a forceful spray of water from the garden hose. Make sure your roses are not crowded and receive good air circulation as plants under stress are often the first to be attacked. Be sure to inspect plants regularly to prevent new infestations from developing. Keep beds around the roses free of leaf litter and debris to eliminate hiding places for the mites.

Rose Gall Wasps

DESCRIPTION: Rose gall wasps vary in size from species to species, but all are extremely difficult to see without the aid of a magnifying glass. These wasplike insects often go unnoticed until after damage has been done.

DAMAGE: In spring, minute adult gall wasps lay their eggs in the stems of roses. After several days the eggs hatch and the larvae begin feeding. The plant reacts to this invasion by producing masses of tissue surrounding the larvae, causing large wartlike swellings, or galls. Galls can be smooth or covered with spines. These unsightly swellings interfere with the plant's ability to absorb water and nutrients, and if left unchecked they reduce the overall health and vigor of the rose.

LIFE HISTORY. Rose gall wasps overwinter in the protective galls. Once the temperature warms in spring, these annoying insects pupate. Later in the summer, the adult wasps eats holes through the galls, emerge and lay eggs. One generation occurs each year.

ECO-FRIENDLY CONTROL: Because these insects are difficult to see, it is a good idea to regularly inspect your roses for galls. If any are present, prune out and destroy infested stems.

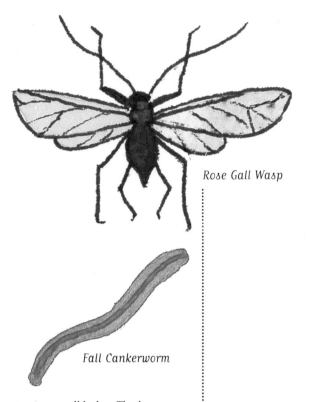

Rose Gall Wasp

Fall Cankerworm

Fall Cankerworms

DESCRIPTION: Fall cankerworm gets its name from the moths that take to the wing only in the fall. Male moths have a wingspan of about 1.25" (30 mm). The forewings are brownish gray with two light bands. The wings behind are light brown with tiny spots. Female moths are wingless and dark gray. Larvae are about 1" (25 mm) long and vary in color from light green to brownish green with a dark stripe on the back. The pupae are oval-shaped, brown and enclosed in cocoons.

DAMAGE: Fall cankerworm larvae feed on the young leaves of roses,

causing small holes. The larvae continue to feed until all the leaf tissue has been eaten.

LIFE HISTORY: In late September and October, moths emerge from their cocoons in the soil. After mating, females lay their eggs in masses of about one hundred eggs on the branches of plants. The eggs overwinter and hatch in spring. After several weeks of feeding, the larvae sometimes spin a web to drop to the ground and move to another plant. Once they are fully grown, they drop to the ground to seek shelter for the winter. There is usually one generation of fall cankerworms for prairie gardeners to worry about.

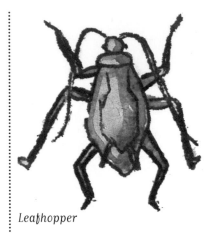

Leafhopper

ECO-FRIENDLY CONTROL: Small infestations of this insect in the larvae stage can be removed with a gloved hand. Eggs can also be removed by hand. Remove and destroy all leaf litter and debris to discourage overwintering.

Leafhoppers

DESCRIPTION: Leafhoppers are about .25" (6 mm) long. They are slender insects whose color may be pale to medium green, yellow or white. These sap-sucking insects are difficult to get a close look at because they jump or hop away when disturbed.

DAMAGE: Damage is caused by both the nymphs and adults, which pierce the leaves and suck out the chlorophyll. Small, yellowish white spots are visible on the leaves, which fall prematurely. Plants will become stunted. Pale mottled skins of leafhoppers may be found on the undersides of leaves.

LIFE HISTORY: Some species of leafhoppers overwinter as adults in protected places, such as leaf litter and debris. Other species migrate from southern regions. In spring, adults emerge to feed on leaves and lay eggs in the leaf tissue.

ECO-FRIENDLY CONTROL: Remove leaf litter and debris that serve as hiding places for overwintering eggs. Avoid overcrowding roses, and keep them in good health as leafhoppers can spread viral diseases. Inspect your roses regularly for damage, and remove and destroy infected leaves.

COMMON DISEASES
Black Spot

DAMAGE: Round black spots are visible on the leaves, stems and leaf stalks. These spots enlarge, grow together and develop yellow margins. Entire leaves turn yellow and drop from the plant. Severely infected roses can lose all their leaves.

LIFE HISTORY: Black spot is caused by a fungus that overwinters on stems and infected leaf residue. This disease becomes more active during warm, wet summer weather. Within a couple of weeks of a black spot appearing on a leaf, spores are produced and the infection is spread by rain or water to other leaves and plants.

ECO-FRIENDLY CONTROL: Choose disease-resistant roses, and carefully inspect for symptoms before planting. Plant roses where they will receive plenty of sun and good air circulation. Prune to maintain an open growth form. Remove and destroy all fallen leaves from infected plants. Persian Yellow, although it's stunning in bloom, is very susceptible to black spot.

Powdery Mildew

DAMAGE: Powdery mildew is a fungal disease appearing on the surface of leaves as blisterlike areas covered with a grayish white powder or mold. Avoid touching these powdery areas, which will disperse large numbers of spores. Symptoms of powdery mildew include stunted growth, distorted leaves and buds, yellow leaves, premature leaf drop and a general decline in plant vigor.

LIFE HISTORY: Powdery mildew is common in crowded plantings where air circulation is poor. Fungi overwinter on diseased stems, fallen leaves and dormant buds. Spores are dispersed by wind and rain.

ECO-FRIENDLY CONTROL: Choose mildew-tolerant or resistant cultivars. Space roses according to their mature size to avoid overcrowding and allow good air circulation. Prune to maintain open growth form. Prune off and destroy infected parts.

Crown Gall

DAMAGE: Crown gall is a bacterial disease that appears as large, rough, tumorlike growths on the canes of roses near the soil level. Infected roses become stunted, and the health of the plant declines.

LIFE HISTORY: This disease enters the plants through pruning and mechanical injuries. Galls enlarge as the numerous spores inside them increase.

ECO-FRIENDLY CONTROL: Avoid injuring plants with garden tools. If crown gall is present, prune off and destroy infected parts.

Canker

DAMAGE: Cankers appear as distinct brown or orange sunken areas on rose branches. The edges of the canker are sometimes swollen, and the bark around the infected area is cracked and dead-looking.

LIFE HISTORY: Canker is a fungal disease that enters the stem through a wound caused by insect damage, pruning or mechanical injury. If left unchecked the canker will enlarge and the growth above the diseased area will die.

ECO-FRIENDLY CONTROL: Avoid injuring plants with garden tools. Use clean sharp tools for pruning to avoid tearing live wood. Avoid leaving any stubs when pruning as these are an open invitation to diseases. Prune out and destroy all the infected wood.

Rust

DAMAGE: Rose rust first appears as small, pale yellow spots on the upper surfaces of leaves in the spring. Later, these spots enlarge, and orange or black pustules appear on the undersides of the

Other Rose Problems
Healthy, vigorous roses make heavy demands on the soil. If you've neglected to amend your soil with well-aged manure or compost before planting, the leaves of your roses may turn yellow. In Chinook regions of the prairies, rugosa roses

leaves. Numerous spots may occur under cool humid conditions.

LIFE HISTORY: Rust is a fungal disease that overwinters in the leaf tissue to produce spores in spring.

ECO-FRIENDLY CONTROL: To pre-

vent additional infection, remove and destroy infected foliage from plants and from the ground around the roses. Adding a new layer of compost or mulch will help prevent the spores from being dispersed.

Powdery Mildew

Rust

Black Spot

Canker

Crown Gall

tend to be more prone to yellowing, which is called chlorosis and may be caused by a deficiency of iron, manganese or nitrogen in the soil. It is not too late to amend the soil after a few yellow leaves have been noticed. Severe chlorosis may require a soil test to determine soil quality before amending.

APPENDIX 1

THE ACCOMPANYING LIST of prairie hardy roses includes those that are readily available in garden centers and from specialty growers. Although many others are available in commerce, I have included ones that are especially well suited to the prairie climate and that represent a range of colors, forms, heights and spreads.

COMMON NAME	HEIGHT	SPREAD	BLOSSOM	COLOR	FRAGRANT
Rosa arkansana					
Adelaide Hoodless	3' (1 M)	3' (1 M)	semi-double to double	dark red	yes
Assiniboine	3' (1 M)	3' (1 M)	semi-double	reddish purple	yes
Cuthbert Grant	2.25' (.75 M)	2.25' (.75 M)	semi-double	dark red	yes
Rosa blanda					
Betty Bland	4.5' (1.5 M)	4.5' (1.5 M)	double	light pink	yes
Rosa foetida					
Austrian Copper	6' (2 M)	6' (2 M)	single	coppery red	no
Persian Yellow	6' (2 M)	6' (2 M)	double	yellow	no
Harison's Yellow	6' (2 M)	6' (2 M)	double	yellow	no
Rosa glauca					
Carmenetta	4.5' (1.5 M)	4.5' (1.5 M)	single	medium pink	yes

RECURRENT	DISEASE SUSCEPTIBILITY	HARDINESS ZONE	COMMENTS	COMMON NAME
yes	BS–1	2	extended bloom period, effective planted *en masse*	Adelaide Hoodless
blooms in July then sporadic till fall	BS–1	2	withstands some drought, effective planted *en masse*	Assiniboine
blooms in July and late summer	BS–1	2	effective planted *en masse*	Cuthbert Grant
yes	BS–1	2	strong arching stems	Betty Bland
blooms in early summer	BS–3	2	strong arching stems, attractive red hips, fine textured foliage with yellow centers	Austrian Copper
blooms in early summer	BS–3	2	fragrant foliage, showy against brown or cedar walls	Persian Yellow
blooms in early summer	BS–3	2	strong arching stems, black hips, called the "Yellow Rose of Texas"	Harison's Yellow
blooms heavily in early summer then sporadic till frost	BS–0	2	arching purplish canes, attractive red winter bark, purplish foliage	Carmenetta

SUSCEPTIBILITY TO BLACK SPOT:
BS–0 : Immune or so little susceptibility as to be insignificant
BS–1 : Generally affecting less that 25% of leaves
BS–2 : Generally affecting more that 25% of leaves

Common Name	Height	Spread	Blossom	Color	Fragrant
Rosa rugosa					
Agnes	3.5' (1.2 M)	3.5' (1.2 M)	double	yellow	yes
Blanc Double de Coubert	4.5' (1.5 M)	4.5' (1.5 M)	double	white	yes
Charles Albanel	20" (50 cm)	3' (1 M)	double	medium red	yes
Dart's Dash	3' (1 M)	3' (1 M)	semi-double	purple	yes
David Thompson	3' (1 M)	3' (1 M)	double	dark pink	yes
Delicata	3' (1 M)	3' (1 M)	semi-double	lilac pink	yes
F.J. Grootendorst	3' (1 M)	3' (1 M)	double	red	no
Fru Dagmar Hastrup	3' (1 M)	3' (1 M)	single	light pink	yes
George Vancouver	3' (1 M)	3' (1 M)	semi-double	medium red	yes
George Will	3' (1 M)	3' (1 M)	double	lilac pink	yes
Grootendorst Supreme	4.5' (1.5 M)	3' (1 M)	double	dark red	no

RECURRENT	DISEASE SUSCEPTIBILITY	HARDINESS ZONE	COMMENTS	COMMON NAME
blooms in July then sporadic until fall	BS–O	2	effective near blue delphiniums	Agnes
yes	BS–O	2	effective in all-white and evening gardens, orange winter hips	Blanc Double de Coubert
yes	BS–O	2	suitable as a ground cover or bordering flower and shrub beds	Charles Albanel
yes	BS–O	2	suitable for flower and shrub beds and as a hedge	Dart's Dash
yes	BS–O	2	suitable for flower and shrub beds and as a hedge	David Thompson
yes	BS–O	2	effective near dark blue perennials	Delicata
yes	BS–I	2	showy near yellow potentillas	F.J. Grootendorst
yes	BS–O	2	attractive winter hips	Fru Dagmar Hastrup
yes	BS–O	2	effective planted *en masse*	George Vancouver
yes	BS–I	2	effective in flower beds, near pathways	George Will
yes	BS–I	2	showy near blue delphiniums	Grootendorst Supreme

Common Name	Height	Spread	Blossom	Color	Fragrant
Hansa	6' (2 M)	6' (2 M)	double	purplish red	yes
Henry Hudson	3' (1 M)	3' (1 M)	semi-double	white	yes
Jens Munk	3' (1 M)	3' (1 M)	semi-double	lavender pink	yes
Martin Frobisher	4.5' (1.5 M)	3' (1 M)	double	pale pink	yes
Mrs. Anthony Waterer	3' (1 M)	3' (1 M)	double	dark red	yes
Rosa x Paulii	3' (1 M)	6' (2 M)	single	white	yes
Pink Grootendorst	4.5' (1.5 M)	3' (1 M)	double	dark pink	no
Pierette Pavement	2.25' (.75 M)	2.25' (.75 M)	semi-double	pale pink	yes
Pink Pavement	2.25' (.75 M)	2.25' (.75 M)	semi-double	salmon rose	yes
Pristine Pavement	3' (1 M)	3' (1 M)	semi-double	white	yes
Purple Pavement	3' (1 M)	3' (1 M)	semi-double	purplish red	yes
Sarah Van Fleet	3' (1 M)	3' (1 M)	semi-double	medium pink	yes
Scarlet Pavement	2.25' (.75 M)	2.25' (.75 M)	semi-double	red	yes
Showy Pavement	2.25' (.75 M)	2.25' (.75 M)	semi-double	pink	yes

RECURRENT	DISEASE SUSCEPTIBILITY	HARDINESS ZONE	COMMENTS	COMMON NAME
yes	BS—O	2	clove-scented flowers, effective in large shrub bed and as a hedge	Hansa
yes	BS—O	2	effective in all-white and evening gardens	Henry Hudson
yes	BS—O	2	bright green wrinkled foliage, showy in perennial beds	Jens Munk
yes	BS—O	2	showy in foundation plantings	Martin Frobisher
yes	BS—O	2	effective near yellow perennials	Mrs. Anthony Waterer
blooms in early summer	BS—O	2	effective ground cover	Rosa x Paulii
yes	BS—O	2	flowers resemble carnations	Pink Grootendorst
yes	BS—O	2	spreading habit	Pierette Pavement
yes	BS—O	2	effective planted *en masse*	Pink Pavement
yes	BS—O	2	attractive shiny foliage	Pristine Pavement
yes	BS—O	2	effective planted *en masse*	Purple Pavement
yes	BS—I	2	ideal for flower and shrub beds	Sarah Van Fleet
yes	BS—O	2	numerous dark-red hips	Scarlet Pavement
yes	BS—O	2	low arching branches	Showy Pavement

COMMON NAME	HEIGHT	SPREAD	BLOSSOM	COLOR	FRAGRANT
Snow Pavement	3' (1 M)	3' (1 M)	semi-double	white	yes
Thérèse Bugnet	6' (2 M)	4.5' (1.5 M)	double	dark pink	yes
White Pavement	2.25' (.75 M)	2.25' (.75 M)	semi-double	white	yes
Rosa spinosissima					
Altai	4.5' (1.5 M)	4.5' (1.5 M)	single	white	yes
Hazeldean	4.5' (1.5 M)	4.5' (1.5 M)	semi-double	yellow	yes
Stanwell Perpetual	3.5' (1.2 M)	3.5' (1.2 M)	double	light pink	yes
MISCELLANEOUS ROSES					
Alexander Mackenzie	4.5' (1.5 M)	4.5' (1.5 M)	double	medium red	yes
Captain Samuel Holland	6' (2 M)	6' (2 M)	double	medium red	yes
Champlain	3' (1 M)	3' (1 M)	semi-double	dark red	yes
Frontenac	3' (1 M)	3' (1 M)	semi-double	dark pink	yes
Henry Kelsey	6' (2 M)	3' (1 M)	semi-double	dark red	yes
John Cabot	6' (2 M)	3' (1 M)	double	medium red	yes

Recurrent	Disease Susceptibility	Hardiness Zone	Comments	Common Name
yes	BS—O	2	effective planted *en masse*	Snow Pavement
yes	BS—O	2	vase-shaped, attractive red winter bark	Thérèse Bugnet
yes	BS—O	2	attractive light-red hips	White Pavement
blooms in early summer then sporadic till fall	BS—O	2	fine-textured foliage, effective in all-white gardens	Altai
blooms in early summer then sporadic till fall	BS—I	2	effective near blue perennials	Hazeldean
yes	BS—O	2	effective in shrub beds and as a hedge	Stanwell Perpetual
yes	BS—O	2	effective as a hedge	Alexander Mackenzie
yes	BS—O	2	effective against arbors, trellises	Captain Samuel Holland
yes	BS—O	2	showy in flower borders	Champlain
yes	BS—O	2	stunning in perennial beds	Frontenac
yes	BS—I	2	effective against arbors, trellises	Henry Kelsey
yes	BS—I	2	effective against arbors, trellises	John Cabot

Common Name	Height	Spread	Blossom	Color	Fragrant
John Davis	4.5' (1.5 M)	4.5' (1.5 M)	double	medium pink	yes
John Franklin	3.5' (1.2 M)	3.5' (1.2 M)	double	medium red	yes
J.P. Connell	3' (1 M)	3' (1 M)	double	yellow	yes
Louis Jolliet	4.5' (1.5 M)	4.5' (1.5 M)	double	medium pink	yes
Marie Bugnet	3' (1 M)	3' (1 M)	double	white	yes
Morden Amorette	3' (1 M)	3' (1 M)	double	red	yes
Morden Blush	3' (1 M)	3' (1 M)	double	pale pink	yes
Morden Cardinette	3' (1 M)	3' (1 M)	double	red	yes
Morden Centennial	3' (1 M)	3' (1 M)	double	medium pink	yes
Morden Fireglow	3' (1 M)	3' (1 M)	semi-double	orange	yes
Morden Ruby	3' (1 M)	3' (1 M)	double	dark pink	yes
Nearly Wild	3' (1 M)	3' (1 M)	single	medium pink	yes
Prairie Dawn	6' (2 M)	6' (2 M)	double	medium pink	yes
Simon Fraser	1.75' (.6 M)	1.75' (.6 M)	double	dark pink	yes
William Baffin	6' (2 M)	3' (1 M)	semi-double	dark pink	yes

Recurrent	Disease Susceptibility	Hardiness Zone	Comments	Common Name
yes	BS—0	2	showy in large shrub bed and as a hedge	John Davis
yes	BS—0	2	flowers are fringed like a carnation	John Franklin
yes	BS—2	2	showy near blue perennials, susceptible to black spot	J.P. Connell
yes	BS—0	2	effective against arbors and as a backdrop for perennials	Louis Jolliet
yes	BS—1	2	effective along pathways	Marie Bugnet
yes	BS—0	2	suitable for massing in beds	Morden Amorette
yes	BS—0	2	suitable for massing in beds	Morden Blush
yes	BS—0	2	suitable for massing in beds	Morden Cardinette
yes	BS—0	2	suitable for massing in beds	Morden Centennial
yes	BS—0	2	showy near blue and yellow perennials	Morden Fireglow
yes	BS—0	2	suitable for massing in beds	Morden Ruby
yes	BS—0	2	nonstop summer bloom, ideal for perennial beds	Nearly Wild
yes	BS—0	2	suitable as a hedge	Prairie Dawn
yes	BS—0	2	perfect as a border plant in flower beds	Simon Fraser
yes	BS—0	2	effective against arbors or trellises	William Baffin

APPENDIX 2
Sources of Hardy Shrub Roses

Alberta Nurseries & Seeds
P.O. Box 20
Bowden, AB
T0M 0K0

Corn Hill Nursery Ltd.
R.R. # 5, Route 890
Petitcodiac, NB
E0A 2H0

Eagle Lake Nurseries
P.O. Box 2340
Strathmore, AB
T1P 1K3

Golden Acre Garden Sentres Ltd.
620 Goddard Avenue NE
Calgary, AB
T2K 5X3

Golden Acre Garden Sentres Ltd.
14111 Macleod Trail SW
Calgary, AB
T2Y 1M6

Hardy Roses for the North
Box 2048CD
Grand Forks, BC
V0H 1H0

Holes Greenhouses
101 Belrose Drive
St. Albert, AB
T8N 1M9

Martin & Kraus
P.O. Box 12
1191 Centre Road
Carlisle, ON
L0R 1H0

McKenzie Seeds
Brandon, MB
R7A 4A4

Pickering Nurseries
670 Kingston Road
Pickering, ON
L1V 1A6

Select Roses
22771 38 Avenue
Langley, BC
V2Z 2G9

Sunnyside Greenhouses
3439 69 Street NW
Calgary, AB
T3B 2J8

T & T Seeds
P.O. Box 1710
Winnipeg, MB
R3C 3P6

Vale's Greenhouse &
Landscape Design
3rd Street NW
Black Diamond, AB
T0L 0H0

INDEX
Plant Name

Entries are filed word by word.

INDEX
General

Entries are filed word by word.

About the Author

JAN MATHER is the owner of Designer Gardens, a landscape design and consulting firm nestled in the heart of the Alberta prairies. Her work has graced prairie landscapes for over a decade, and her horticultural and design expertise has helped thousands of prairie gardeners understand not just

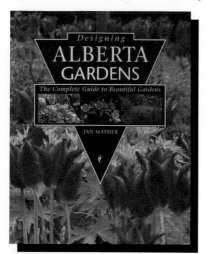

which plants thrive in our unforgiving climate, but what mixes of plants create the most spectacular prairie displays. When she's not busy helping gardeners create their own prairie paradises, she is a gardening columnist for the *Calgary Herald*, a frequent contributor to magazines, and a popular horticultural workshop leader. She also is the bestselling author of *Designing Alberta Gardens* and *The Prairie Garden Planner*.

Praise for Designing Alberta Gardens

"If you attempt to garden in Alberta, this book is a must. Lush, colorful . . . a joy to behold. . . . Full of practical, yet innovative, suggestions which are specifically tailored to the short, finicky growing season here. You'll love this book. It's a keeper." —*Calgary Herald*

"Finally, a garden ideas book that is relevant to our particular climate. . . . A book for those who have contemplated a large expanse of lawn . . . and wondered how to change it, or for those who are bewildered by the selection of plants in Alberta nurseries and what to do with them." —*Edmonton Journal*

"Jan Mather's book provides a much-needed bridge between the art and science of creating beautiful residential gardens suited to the real conditions of the province." —Bernard Amell, Landscape Architect, Calgary

Praise for The Prairie Garden Planner

Best garden planner, 1996. —*Canadian Gardening*

"One of the best purchases most gardeners could make." —*Regina Leader Post*

"The perfect gift for the beginning gardener, or gardener who keeps information on bits of scrap paper tucked into catalogues or books." —*Calgary Herald*

AVAILABLE AT FINE BOOKSTORES AND GARDEN CENTERS ACROSS THE PRAIRIES